View from the Middle of the Road

Where the Greenest Grass Grows

View from the Middle of the Road

Where the Greenest Grass Grows

Poems by Lucinda J. Clark
Contributions by Jessica and Xavier Clark
Edited by Brenda Barratto

P.R.A. Publishing

Poems by Lucinda Clark
Contributions by Jessica and Xavier Clark
Edited by Brenda Barratto

First printing and second printing
P.R.A. Publishing
P.O. Box 211701
Martinez, Georgia 30917
praent2000@yahoo.com

Cover art: *Walking in Faith* is reproduced from an original acrylic painting by
AudreyCrosby©2001. Used with permission of the artist.

Dreamscape I-V. Published January 2004 in Visions, JWM Publishing, USA
Dreamscape I-V. Performed at "For the Love of Art",
Perspectives of a Woman- Atlanta, Ga. 2004
Credit, Bob and Lou, Blazing and Faith. , performed at Sacred Heart Cultural
Center- Augusta, Ga. 2004

This book was printed in the United States of America.

Thanks and love to

Bob, my husband,

Jessica, my daughter

Xavier, my son

God, for all good things come from Him.

Acknowledgments

This book has been no small feat. There have been ups and downs in getting it to press and finally the finished product of which I am extremely proud of. That means all the people who have played a role in making this possible must be recognized.

I would like to thank Audrey Crosby for lending her creative talents in the beautiful artwork which graces the cover of this book. She has been very modest about her talent. She is an artist to watch in the future.

I would also like to thank Brenda Barratto for all of her feedback and editing help.

Bob who is a great poet but doesn't want to show it, encouraging me to write it down has really helped.

My children, Jessica and Xavier; co-authors, muses and traveling companions. The adventures we share make everyday something special. Thanks for your contributions to this book and your youthful wit and wisdom.

My mother-in-law Anna Carter, Anna, we have come a long way in this life journey. Thanks for all the funny stories, long talks and spiritual wisdom.

I would also like to acknowledge my own mother, Mary Johnson. She raised seven children, and worked a full time job while raising a family. She is loved and all her efforts at sharing are appreciated.

My Dad. He told me a long time ago I would write a book. Well Dad, thanks for believing I would do it even before I knew I would.

To my friends, clients, colleagues and associates. This book would not have possible without the experiences and interactions we have shared. My life's journey has been made that much richer because of you all. I have learned that life lessons are all around us; it is only when we chose to open up and share that we can receive the greatest blessings. Thanks!

Table of Contents

First Thoughts

Second Thoughts

Growing Pains

Identity Crisis

Bright Spots on the Road

FIRST THOUGHTS

"The best portions of a good person's life are the little, nameless, unremembered acts of kindness and love"

--William Wordsworth

THE TRUTH ABOUT BEING THE FIRST

I am the first.
To attempt to cross the great barrier.
To survive the crossing
To hold my head and hands high in victory.

I am the only one.
Who represents the many.
Who is a credit to my gender and race.

It is a silent hollow victory
A victory that is never spoken aloud or
in mixed company.

In some people's mind,
I am a fluke
An anomaly
An abomination.

All I know
I am alone.

MENTAL ILLNESS

It comes like a thief in the night
Silent
Carrying larceny in its heart

It sometimes comes as a bearer of gifts.
The very model of humbleness.
Perhaps, it is disguised in a request
Even as a favor.

It can slip in oh so gradually
With an offer of assistance or
A tale of woe.

It begins to consume you
With its petty problems,
Troublesome friends,
Ungrateful family members
Unacknowledged acts of kindness

Then BAM!

Before you know it
You are depressed.
Constantly worried.

Afraid of everyone and everything,
Paralyzed by the sudden onset of darkness.
The intense feelings of hatred and despair.

You notice
Your friends no longer call you
Your family becomes deeply disturbed
by the sudden change in your
mood.

You find it difficult to speak up.
To cry for help,
To seek guidance or understanding.
Instead you succumb to the sinister specter
that now robs you of your soul.

SECRETS

It began as sadness
A sudden tragedy occurred.
For which you were blamed.

It escalated into fear.
Because you had no one
to reassure you everything would be O.K.

Fear became anger.
Anger, because you could
not run away.
There was no place to go.
Now anger is rage.
The most hideous of cancers.

It drives a wedge into everything.
It consumes every ounce of happiness
It allows no joy, light or love.

If you could only let love reach you.
It surrounds you everyday
Believe the universe conspires
To give only happiness.
Look for the light of love and prosperity

The darkness will soon go away.

IS MY COLOR THE REASON?

Rude salesperson
Inconsiderate waiter
Is it because of my color?

Don't know.
Could be the person is just rude and
inconsiderate.

Depending on with whom I am traveling
in any of these situations.
The response to this query would be different.

If I am with my parents.
Our plight stems from being black

If I am with white friends there is
no mistreatment.
the person in question is obviously;
tired, in a hurry or just having a bad day.

If I am with my black friends
any of the above responses is possible.

If I am with my children,
All responses must make reference to people who do not
like their jobs.

Which perspective is right, true?
I say it is the one that does not
blame my color.
For my mistreatment.

DEAR DR. KING

Two score and two years ago,
my parents bore a darling baby girl.
Me.

Seven years later,
You were taken from this earth.
But, you left us your dream.

Now, thirty five years later,
I would like to share with you
what has gone on since your passing.

You are an international hero.
Only three other people have reached your
stature and renown.
Nelson Mandela, Sister Teresa and
Princess Diana.

We are called African American now.
We head Fortune 500 companies,
We sit on corporation boards,
We dominate golf, tennis and baseball.

Our music still shapes American culture.
It's called hip-hop now.
All this, yet some would say
we are not living your dream.

This comes after the community destroying riots
of the 60's, 70's and 80's.
The ravages of crack, Aids and incarceration
on many of our brethren.
The fall of some leaders that may surprise you.

Even with all this despair,
Our future still looks bright because of you
Dr. King.

Your dream still inspires,
Every third Monday in January
Our country stops business and takes pause.
We are reminded and motivated anew.

Thank you!

CREDIT

When actively sought,
it will elude you
or
backfire.

When desired with all your heart,
every action taken to get it,
turns nightmarish or causes pain.
Whether intentional or not.

When stolen,
it causes resentment and acts of revenge
to hound you.
For the forces of karmic and spiritual law
have been activated.

When hogged,
desired outcomes are diminished.
The applause personal pride receives.
Is overshadowed by the hunger for truth
that remains in the soul.

When shared,
a light shines like a thousand suns,
not blinding but warming through and
through.

When given freely,
In all things great and small
a chain reaction occurs.
First the recipient grows.
Second, the giver grows
third the act becomes contagious.

The idea that it is better to give than
to receive is allowed to come
full circle.

For credit is only valuable.
If it is used well
and preserved.

A MISUNDERSTANDING CLARIFIED

She was taught,
She could do anything she wanted to.
She just needed a good education.

Her teachers forgot to mention,
how expensive a good education can be
and that no funds would be forthcoming.
She got a decent education anyway.

She was taught,
She must be three times as good,
Just to be considered an equal.

She worked three times as hard
And found,
That being equal was just a matter of perspective.

She was taught,
The world in which she would travel,
Will never see her as good enough,
No matter how good she got at anything.

She learned.
That she must always do her best
and that that, should be good enough.

She was taught.
To succeed, she would have to be strong.
Stronger than a tall sturdy oak tree.

She learned,
that with such strength,
she could also be broken, never to rise again.
Just like that same oak tree is broken in a fierce wind.

She was taught.
She must concern herself with comments
and criticisms from others.

She learned,
while feedback is constructive
to thy own self be true.

SECOND THOUGHTS

Two roads diverged in a wood, and I
I took the one less traveled by
And that has made all the difference.

--Robert Frost

MORNING REFLECTION

The time
Early morning,
Filled with peaceful silence
A glorious chill fills the air
Thoughts of all that must be done today
Replaced with humble gratitude.

The Sky
Bright and star filled
One cloud
Appears to streak
In and out of the stratosphere.

O how grand is the universe
How small and insignificant am I.

DREAMSCAPE I-V

As baby girls
We dream BIG!

As little girls we look to life to confirm
And validate those dreams.

As teenagers,
Our dreams become cloudy and confused,
From the haze of hormones,
Peer pressure and advertising.

As young adults,
Our dreams begin to conform
To the "norms" of our society.

For some women, this is the start
Of real confusion.
For in a patriarchal society,
There is always a better plan for us.

Our big dreams now,
Seem like figments of our imagination.
What was that big dream I had?
O yes, to nurture the future dreamers.
No more dreaming for myself.

As middle aged women,
Sometimes the dream tries to come back,
however, based on how well the dreamer
has conformed to her accepted role
in society

The dream may remain locked in the closet
of "when the kids get older".

The potential dreamer becomes
a multi-tasking cheerleader.
Cheering on the never ending stream of:
Husband's dreams
Children's dreams
Aging parents needs
and so on.

And the cycle continues......

As elderly women,
Beauty fading and child rearing over.
There is one last moment of truth.
Do we dare live our big dream?

OR

Become the nurturers of the next,
next generation?
Only to find in the end,
We slept fitfully through our lives.

NEW ATTITUDES

Today's society has fallen
into a shattered and torn
shadow of what once was.

In a male dominated world the reason for this is simple.

Some men say,

*"Women are refusing to stay in their
proper place
They would, heaven forbid,
work and make a contribution to our world".
"They want to have voices which are all their own".
They no longer find comfort
in being wives and mothers only"*

These patriarchs believe,
They have bestowed upon women,
the greatest of honors,
To be kept and cared for.
To appreciate the importance
of unwavering *service.*

Some women say,

*I will serve, not as a sacrificial lamb.
but in partnership,
A dynamic relationship,
that strives for the betterment of all.
These are the new terms of engagement.*

How does this new attitude affect
the innocent by-standers, our children?
Depends, on the child's gender.

Boys can now say,

"It's okay to share all aspects of my life
to be a partner in spirit and through my actions".

Girls can now say,

"I don't have to feel guilty about trying to have it all"

Both genders are learning
by example.
That a person's place in the world
is determined by choice.
Not by gender.

Does that make for the decline of a society?

No, that would be the job of television.

MARTYRS

She pines away,
giving away the best years
of her life.

Never realizing that in the truest sense
A martyr must die for a cause,
before she can be held up, revered.

To sacrifice your dreams willingly
does not a martyr make.
What it does, is make for a whining sour puss
Who demands reverence by force or threat.
The sad truth is, there are never any revelers
not for long anyway.

All the long suffering Madonna has done is made
a lifestyle decision.

To all the long-suffering Madonnas:

Remember
A life lived with no regret
is a life lived well.
So be held high for being true to yourself.

Do that which, you know
The creator has called on you to do.
stop trying to make the
rest of the world feel guilty, sad or pity
for what you lacked the courage
to do.

LUNCHTIME CONVERSATION

One day at lunch with a friend
I was accused of having a life
my companion should have had.

Perplexed by the teary eyed forcefulness
of the statement.
I tried to figure out what
my accuser meant.

Was she entitled to my parents, siblings and friends?
My life choices?
My husband and children?

Did she expect me to apologize
for all the hard work, soul searching
and planning done to get where I am?

After several moments in
silent contemplation.
I had an answer for my friend.

No, you should not have my life
You should live happily and proactively in your own.

Go back and acknowledge
with simple joy and gratitude as I have
Every aspect of what sounds like
a life lived in despair.

And be glad for what good can be found in
your own life.
For the life of another always looks greener
from the other side.

WAKE– UP CALL

I awoke one morning
With a strong sense of longing
in my heart.

I have everything.
A great family
A great house
A great car
Accomplishment and renown

Yet somehow it all seems
shallow and empty,
Materialistic and over done.

For spiritually I have been shaken
Physically weaken from pondering the question,
What have they done?

It was in that very moment
A realization did come.
That the world has many illusions
And now I have none.

A WHISPER TURNS

So much to do for so many others
in so little time.

When do I make time for myself?
If spoken aloud this would be a selfish thought
I could be as labeled self-absorbed.

So the thought is quickly stifled,
with body and mind numbing activity
self chastising,
preoccupation with the coming and going
of family and friends

Yet.....

With each passing day,
The voice inside begins to clamor ever so loudly.
When will it be our time?
Eventually the preoccupied mind must stop
the unproductive banter and respond.

Right Now!

SOME SISTERS

Some sisters can appreciate
A struggle
sacrifice and pain.
Some sisters can't.

Some sisters can relate
to the confusion, gyrations
and strength required.
Just to get through yet another day.
Some sisters can't.

Some sisters assume,
they are privileged princesses
all powerful and seductive.
In complete control of their world
Some sisters don't

Some sisters understand
and will not tolerate being
underfoot
under the gun or misunderstood.
While some sisters not only tolerate it,
they assume it's their birthright.

In the world of the heralded princess,
baby dolled, second class citizen.
Some sisters sadly take it.
Proudly shouldering the degradation and belittlement.

When will these sisters get it?
It does not require anger.
Just a little self-respect.
Because
We are all queens in our own right
Neither subjects nor objects to anyone.

REACHING OUT/ LOOKING BACK

Oh Where, Oh where,
Have all my sisters gone?

Oh Where. Oh where.
Can they be?
I have looked over yonder
I have searched
high and low
only to find
I have searched in vain.

Searching and seeking
in all the wrong places.
For they are there.
They have been all along.

If only I had looked in the right places
How was I to know I was wrong?

Yet, I have found them.
Silently, steadily
making their way in the world.

Once found.
They received me with open arms.
I had finally made my way back home.

GROWING PAINS

"Every winner has scars"

--Herbert N. Casson

"Blazing"

To blaze a trail
One must recognize at the onset
that is what she is doing.

For it summons the positive forces born of confidence.
Instead of the negative forces born of arrogance.

If one chooses to become a trail blazer
She must be aware,
so that she can prepare
for the wake, that trail blazing inevitably causes:

Lost innocence.
Removal from the comfortable world she now knows.
Change, for her life will never be the same.

What are the final results
if one chooses to blaze a trail?

A pile of ashes.
Of what once was,
blowing forcefully in the wind.

Replaced by something new,
unexpected, different.

Combined with the old trail,
A new trail blazed
Now makes a fork in the road.

FRIDAYS AT THE CIRCUS

For one year
Fridays loomed like a huge cloud
on the horizon.

I would awake on Friday mornings,
head filled with all the things
I did or did not do the Friday before.

I would visualize a three-ring circus,
With

Great feats of wonder
Death defying acts in tow.
Acts of amazing courage
Acts which could stop the heart, you know?

There would be a ritual of suiting up
to shield me from accidental dents.
The stuffing of props into the car.
The drive to the big circus tents.

Upon my arrival ticket takers would greet me
and assist with the steadying of my nerves.
Nourishment would arrive to fortify me.
Sometimes the food and drink had to be deferred.
Because, the spectators and acts would begin to stream in.

Some of the spectators
Arrived happy and friendly.
Others grouchy and grim.
There was never any doubt as the room filled up
That a show was about to begin.

I would stand to clang a bell
this, called the circus to order.

I would think to myself,
In one hour another
Friday at the circus will end.

And I, the lady ringmaster.
Just had to hold it all together until then.

NATURE TO LIFE

It is like the weather.
It is governed by the seasons.

It is like spring, sometimes hot
sometimes cold, everything green
young, teeming, with promise.

It is like summer
A summer day in Georgia
blindingly bright, stifling heat, unrelenting
Everything maturing
some things of the youthful spring
giving way to stabilizing influences.

It is like fall,
Cool and colorful,
Warning of the barren winter to come.
everything changing, preparing for first frost.
The final shedding of all things of
a spring fulfilled youth.

It is like winter.
With its beautiful sunsets
So moving they take your breath away,
only to quickly chill, after the sun vanishes
from the horizon.
A time when some things
go away for good.
To make way for the new.

LIARS, WHEN THEY FINALLY SPEAK THE TRUTH, ARE NOT BELIEVED

It was written on a fortune cookie.
In small red and white letters.

Found in a moment,
A turning point
A weekly house cleaning.

As the arrival of a visitor
was being contemplated.
Oh what pain this person has caused.
The memories reemerge after being
submerged by years of self therapy,
prayers and acts of desperation.

The turning point could not have been more
Fortunate
Spiritual
Prophetic

It may have literally saved a life.

FULL CIRCLE

I saw you today
after many years.
You looked the same,
except you now have
a few more wrinkles and pounds.

You immediately recall an act of injustice.
Performed by your hand against me,
I struggle to recall the details
I forgive you again.

You want to make sure
everything is okay now.
You ask again how it is going.
You insist that I come by and visit
You ask again, if I am still mad.

Everything is fine.
For you see the injustice
did not hinder me
It did not deter or deflate
the focus of my goal
It only took your contribution out
of the equation.

To see now that forgiveness and forward movement
were indeed the right action
There is now confirmation
That all actions, words and deeds become a part of
A life long circle

That
Eventually,
Revisits each of us.
Our reactions upon the revisit
Are based purely
On what lessons we may have
learned.

This day brings new insight.
You have a conscience
And I the capacity to forgive.

IDENTITY CRISIS

" Be yourself. Imitation is suicide"

--Marva Collins

WHERE DOES THE GREENEST GRASS GROW?

When someone decides
to look for happiness,
Where does he look for it?
In the urban wastelands?
Full of massive diversity, distrust,
physical and moral decay?

Or

In a peaceful rural setting
Where living is cheap and easy.
Where grass grows
Birds sing and
the stars shine brightly in the night sky?

When one decides to raise a family
Where does she look?
To the big city lights?
With its promise of never ending activity?
Full of throngs of faces and places
guaranteed to overwhelm the senses?

Or

Does she look in the country?
Where excitement is found in a solitary venture.
Where the closest neighbor is at least a mile away.
No crushing rush hour panic.
No buses, trolleys or planes.
To sing her a nighttime lullaby.

When one looks to embrace his culture,
does he turn to the prepackaged definition
of his culture, mass marketed by the media,
with its ultimate goal of making a sale?

Or
Does he look to the vivid recollections,
found in quiet sit downs
with living members of generations past?

When one is said to be a credit to his race.
Does he?
Make a list of his ancestors?
The known with the possible unknowns?
Checking boxes that closely resemble
his skin tone, eyes and other facial features?

Or

Does he shrug off being "culturally correct"
and just embrace the race he is most
familiar with?

What happens if we ignore our
socio-economic standing,
our color, gender, region of origin,
and religious affiliation?

Alas, we cannot because
it is who we are
and with that, we must do that,
which feels comfortable, compatible
and right for us as individuals.

Seeking acceptance in a sometimes
crazy but beautiful world.

NOTHING LEFT TO PROVE

We have journeyed,
beyond the great wall of ignorance.
Taken on the challenge
of the raging oceans of strangers
emotions to our very presence
and survived.

We have carried the great burden.
Pulled off our weighted shackles.
Climbed to the top of the mountain
and victoriously stood.

We have witnessed and
cried out over injustices.
Paid our dues
over and over.

We have fought
for the cause
and now.

We stand.
Heads unbowed
bruised to the depths of our souls.
Eyes fixed on the horizon.
Satisfied.
We have nothing left
to prove.

BOB AND LOU

They met in the city,
on the stairs of an
apartment fire escape.
Lou, a budding entrepreneur
Bob, a dashing doctor- to- be.

Bob approached Lou with confidence
He was new to the building
and in need of aid.

They met courted and married.
Out of the union came two children.
A baby girl, who struggled for life
from the moment of her birth.
Then a baby boy, who was healthy as a horse.

The four of them travel the road of life.
Bob, a successful doctor
Lou, a mother, entrepreneur
and wife.
The kids grew, both are now
the source of Bob and Lou's
delight.

The moral of this poem:
Finding the right partner in life can
be the one thing
that makes life's travels in hindsight,
appear miraculous, spectacular and right.
Combined in the present, it is what keeps your future
outlook bright.

FAITH

Faith is the difference
between belief and being.

It is the lighthouse,
which cast a beacon of light and hope
over the darkest, stormy sea.

It is the action
one takes without questioning
why or what for.

It is the stillness that comes
over everything,
during a violent quake.

True faith
is never tested
never questioned
It just is.

We are only left to
experience its power,
to bring sunshine even after
the darkest of days.

INNER PEACE AT LAST

The external world
clamors for our attention.
Everywhere one looks there are
suffering adults, animals and children,
countless victims of ever increasing
tragedy.

We are told
the way to serenity can be found
by giving.

So we give
Frantically, telling ourselves as we do.
That our wells will never run dry.
Until one day.

We stand motionless,
simply unable to move.
our energy drained
our pockets almost empty
our hopes fading.

Then a miracle occurs.
an unselfish act of kindness
is done for us.

It is in that moment
we can truly understand
inner peace.

For inner peace is a circle
that can only be kept going
by faith.

Once Upon A Time

Use to be able
to eat anything
at anytime
and never notice a thing.

Now

Some of those same foods give
heartburn, headaches and
where the calories
settle.
Let's not even go there.

Use to remember
the names and personal stats
on every person,
I ever met.

Now

The last place I put
my car keys takes up
most of that space.

I use to
read the letters on a page
with the eyes of a hawk.

Now

I stare down the aisles
in the supermarket
trying to find a product
that was there only yesterday.

Only to have a stock clerk
point it out.
I put on my reading glasses
There it is. Why did I have doubt?
I use to be greeted
with slang and liked it.

What's up girl?
What's happening?

Now

I hear
Good Afternoon Mrs.?
How are you Mrs.?
and I don't even mind.

It may be a shift in thinking
It may be the changing times.

Do I accept the label
"Baby Boomer "relegated
to middle aged?

Or simply state the obvious,
that a lot of years have gone by
and that this is just the next phrase.

Either way you slice it.
Youth as I remember it,
has seen better days.

BRIGHT SPOTS ON THE ROAD

*I shall be in this world but once. Any good I can do
or any kindness I can show any human being
let me do it now and not defer it.
For I shall not pass this way again.*

Unknown

THANK YOU
By Jessica Clark

Thank you for teaching me,
the skills needed for life
and to survive in the world.

For sharing your ideas and feelings
with me.
For giving me life and knowledge.
For your love, and friendship.
For caring when I was in trouble or sick.
I wish I could express all my feelings
on paper, or in words.

But it is impossible.
Like us being apart.

LAUGHTER IS LIKE
By Jessica Clark

Laughter is yellow
like a sunny day
with light shining on you.

Laughter is like a happy dog
tail wagging.
It flies through my soul.

It reminds me of the time
I saw my mom walk into the room.
It made me burst with joy.

TO MY PARENTS
By Xavier Clark

From the moment of my conception,
to the second in which we stand.

You have always been there to guide me,
there to hold my hand.

Sometimes your annoying habits
may make me twitch and scream
but most times we are all together
It's like a perfect dream.

You may think I'm embarrassed
To be seen in public with you.
Yet, I am always elated
when I'm with you.

Thanks for all the gifts
and happiness you have brought
I truly love you both.

About the Author

Lucinda Clark is the founder of P.R.A. Publishing. She has worked with visual artists and authors on the protection, promotion and marketing of their creative works for the past seventeen years.

Clark has sponsored and judged numerous art and writing contest for school aged children throughout her career. She is a co-founding member of the CSRA Poetry Society. She is also a member of the American Academy of Poets and the Georgia Poetry Society. She has lived in New Orleans, La. where she studied and received both her Bachelor of Science and Master degrees from Dillard and Tulane Universities. She also completed her legal studies with British American University School of Law in 2003.

Lucinda currently resides in Martinez, Georgia with her husband and two contributing author children, Jessica and Xavier.

About the Artist

Audrey Marie Crosby has loved painting and drawing since early childhood. She is by and large a self-taught artist. She is currently a part-time curator at the Lucy Craft Laney Museum in Augusta, Ga. She holds a Bachelor of Business Administration degree from Tennessee State University. She has won numerous honors and awards for her art work in both Memphis Tennessee and Augusta, Georgia since moving to Augusta in 1995. Her work can be found in both private and museums collections. She has been showcased in numerous print periodicals and has gallery representation in Augusta, Georgia.

Audrey currently resides in Augusta with her husband and son.

www.ingramcontent.com/pod-product-compliance
Lightning Source LLC
Chambersburg PA
CBHW051738040426
42447CB00008B/1202